WE'RE HAPPY YOU'RE HERE!

Our Location Information

NARIKU
Publishing

Copyright © 2020 by Nariku Publishing

For more information: narikupublishing@gmail.com

Imagery courtesy of Canva.com

WELCOME

May all who come as guests leave as friends.

Guest Names

_____

_____

_____

_____

_____

Dates of Stay

_____

_____

Traveled From

_____

_____

Doodles and Drawings

Message to Host

_____

_____

_____

_____

_____

_____

_____

_____

_____

Favorite Places to Go and Things to Do

_____

_____

_____

_____

_____

Special Moments and Highlights of Our Stay

_____

_____

_____

_____

_____

_____

Guest Names

Dates of Stay

Traveled From

Doodles and Drawings

Message to Host

Favorite Places to Go and Things to Do

Special Moments and Highlights of Our Stay

Guest Names

_____

_____

_____

_____

_____

Dates of Stay

_____

_____

Traveled From

_____

_____

_____

Doodles and Drawings

Message to Host

_____

_____

_____

_____

_____

_____

_____

_____

_____

_____

Favorite Places to Go and Things to Do

_____

_____

_____

_____

_____

_____

Special Moments and Highlights of Our Stay

_____

_____

_____

_____

_____

_____

Guest Names

Dates of Stay

Traveled From

Doodles and Drawings

Message to Host

Favorite Places to Go and Things to Do

Special Moments and Highlights of Our Stay

Guest Names

Dates of Stay

Traveled From

Doodles and Drawings

Message to Host

Favorite Places to Go and Things to Do

Special Moments and Highlights of Our Stay

Guest Names

Dates of Stay

Traveled From

Doodles and Drawings

Message to Host

Favorite Places to Go and Things to Do

Special Moments and Highlights of Our Stay

Guest Names

_____

_____

_____

_____

Dates of Stay

_____

_____

Traveled From

_____

_____

_____

Doodles and Drawings

Message to Host

_____

_____

_____

_____

_____

_____

_____

Favorite Places to Go and Things to Do

_____

_____

_____

_____

_____

Special Moments and Highlights of Our Stay

_____

_____

_____

_____

_____

_____

Guest Names

Dates of Stay

Traveled From

Doodles and Drawings

Message to Host

Favorite Places to Go and Things to Do

Special Moments and Highlights of Our Stay

Guest Names

_____

_____

_____

_____

Dates of Stay

_____

_____

Traveled From

_____

_____

_____

Doodles and Drawings

Message to Host

_____

_____

_____

_____

_____

_____

_____

Favorite Places to Go and Things to Do

_____

_____

_____

_____

_____

_____

Special Moments and Highlights of Our Stay

_____

_____

_____

_____

_____

_____

Guest Names

Dates of Stay

Traveled From

Doodles and Drawings

Message to Host

Favorite Places to Go and Things to Do

Special Moments and Highlights of Our Stay

Guest Names

_____

_____

_____

_____

Dates of Stay

_____

_____

Traveled From

_____

_____

_____

Doodles and Drawings

Message to Host

_____

_____

_____

_____

_____

_____

_____

_____

Favorite Places to Go and Things to Do

_____

_____

_____

_____

_____

_____

Special Moments and Highlights of Our Stay

_____

_____

_____

_____

_____

_____

_____

Guest Names

Dates of Stay

Traveled From

Doodles and Drawings

Message to Host

Favorite Places to Go and Things to Do

Special Moments and Highlights of Our Stay

Guest Names

Dates of Stay

Traveled From

Doodles and Drawings

Message to Host

Favorite Places to Go and Things to Do

Special Moments and Highlights of Our Stay

Guest Names

Dates of Stay

Traveled From

Doodles and Drawings

Message to Host

Favorite Places to Go and Things to Do

Special Moments and Highlights of Our Stay

Guest Names

Dates of Stay

Traveled From

Doodles and Drawings

Message to Host

Favorite Places to Go and Things to Do

Special Moments and Highlights of Our Stay

Guest Names

_____
_____
_____
_____
_____

Dates of Stay

_____
_____

Traveled From

_____
_____
_____

Doodles and Drawings

Message to Host

_____
_____
_____
_____
_____
_____
_____
_____

Favorite Places to Go and Things to Do

_____
_____
_____
_____
_____

Special Moments and Highlights of Our Stay

_____
_____
_____
_____
_____

Guest Names

Dates of Stay

Traveled From

Doodles and Drawings

Message to Host

Favorite Places to Go and Things to Do

Special Moments and Highlights of Our Stay

Guest Names

Dates of Stay

Traveled From

Doodles and Drawings

Message to Host

Favorite Places to Go and Things to Do

Special Moments and Highlights of Our Stay

Guest Names

_____
_____
_____
_____

Dates of Stay

_____
_____

Traveled From

_____
_____

Doodles and Drawings

Message to Host

_____
_____
_____
_____
_____
_____
_____
_____

Favorite Places to Go and Things to Do

_____
_____
_____
_____
_____

Special Moments and Highlights of Our Stay

_____
_____
_____
_____
_____

Guest Names

Dates of Stay

Traveled From

Doodles and Drawings

Message to Host

Favorite Places to Go and Things to Do

Special Moments and Highlights of Our Stay

Guest Names

_____

_____

_____

_____

_____

Dates of Stay

_____

_____

Traveled From

_____

_____

_____

Doodles and Drawings

Message to Host

_____

_____

_____

_____

_____

_____

_____

Favorite Places to Go and Things to Do

_____

_____

_____

_____

_____

Special Moments and Highlights of Our Stay

_____

_____

_____

_____

_____

Guest Names

Dates of Stay

Traveled From

Doodles and Drawings

Message to Host

Favorite Places to Go and Things to Do

Special Moments and Highlights of Our Stay

Guest Names

_____

_____

_____

_____

Dates of Stay

_____

_____

Traveled From

_____

_____

_____

Doodles and Drawings

Message to Host

_____

_____

_____

_____

_____

_____

_____

_____

Favorite Places to Go and Things to Do

_____

_____

_____

_____

_____

_____

Special Moments and Highlights of Our Stay

_____

_____

_____

_____

_____

_____

Guest Names

Dates of Stay

Traveled From

Doodles and Drawings

Message to Host

Favorite Places to Go and Things to Do

Special Moments and Highlights of Our Stay

Guest Names

Dates of Stay

Traveled From

Doodles and Drawings

Message to Host

Favorite Places to Go and Things to Do

Special Moments and Highlights of Our Stay

Guest Names

Dates of Stay

Traveled From

Doodles and Drawings

Message to Host

Favorite Places to Go and Things to Do

Special Moments and Highlights of Our Stay

Guest Names

Dates of Stay

Traveled From

Doodles and Drawings

Message to Host

Favorite Places to Go and Things to Do

Special Moments and Highlights of Our Stay

Guest Names

Dates of Stay

Traveled From

Doodles and Drawings

Message to Host

Favorite Places to Go and Things to Do

Special Moments and Highlights of Our Stay

Guest Names

_____

_____

_____

_____

_____

Dates of Stay

_____

_____

Traveled From

_____

_____

_____

Doodles and Drawings

Message to Host

_____

_____

_____

_____

_____

_____

_____

Favorite Places to Go and Things to Do

_____

_____

_____

_____

_____

_____

Special Moments and Highlights of Our Stay

_____

_____

_____

_____

_____

Guest Names

Dates of Stay

Traveled From

Doodles and Drawings

Message to Host

Favorite Places to Go and Things to Do

Special Moments and Highlights of Our Stay

Guest Names

_____

_____

_____

_____

Dates of Stay

_____

_____

Traveled From

_____

_____

_____

Doodles and Drawings

Message to Host

_____

_____

_____

_____

_____

_____

_____

_____

Favorite Places to Go and Things to Do

_____

_____

_____

_____

_____

Special Moments and Highlights of Our Stay

_____

_____

_____

_____

_____

_____

Guest Names

Dates of Stay

Traveled From

Doodles and Drawings

Message to Host

Favorite Places to Go and Things to Do

Special Moments and Highlights of Our Stay

Guest Names

_____
_____
_____
_____
_____

Dates of Stay

_____
_____

Traveled From

_____
_____
_____

Doodles and Drawings

Message to Host

_____
_____
_____
_____
_____
_____
_____
_____
_____
_____

Favorite Places to Go and Things to Do

_____
_____
_____
_____
_____
_____

Special Moments and Highlights of Our Stay

_____
_____
_____
_____
_____

Guest Names

Dates of Stay

Traveled From

Doodles and Drawings

Message to Host

Favorite Places to Go and Things to Do

Special Moments and Highlights of Our Stay

Guest Names

_____

_____

_____

_____

Dates of Stay

_____

Traveled From

_____

_____

_____

Doodles and Drawings

Message to Host

_____

_____

_____

_____

_____

_____

_____

_____

Favorite Places to Go and Things to Do

_____

_____

_____

_____

_____

Special Moments and Highlights of Our Stay

_____

_____

_____

_____

_____

_____

Guest Names

Dates of Stay

Traveled From

Doodles and Drawings

Message to Host

Favorite Places to Go and Things to Do

Special Moments and Highlights of Our Stay

Guest Names

_____

_____

_____

_____

Dates of Stay

_____

_____

Traveled From

_____

_____

_____

Doodles and Drawings

Message to Host

_____

_____

_____

_____

_____

_____

_____

_____

_____

Favorite Places to Go and Things to Do

_____

_____

_____

_____

_____

_____

Special Moments and Highlights of Our Stay

_____

_____

_____

_____

_____

_____

Guest Names

Dates of Stay

Traveled From

Doodles and Drawings

Message to Host

Favorite Places to Go and Things to Do

Special Moments and Highlights of Our Stay

Guest Names

Dates of Stay

Traveled From

Doodles and Drawings

Message to Host

Favorite Places to Go and Things to Do

Special Moments and Highlights of Our Stay

Guest Names

Dates of Stay

Traveled From

Doodles and Drawings

Message to Host

Favorite Places to Go and Things to Do

Special Moments and Highlights of Our Stay

Guest Names

Dates of Stay

Traveled From

Doodles and Drawings

Message to Host

Favorite Places to Go and Things to Do

Special Moments and Highlights of Our Stay

Guest Names

Dates of Stay

Traveled From

Doodles and Drawings

Message to Host

Favorite Places to Go and Things to Do

Special Moments and Highlights of Our Stay

Guest Names

Message to Host

Dates of Stay

Traveled From

Favorite Places to Go and Things to Do

Doodles and Drawings

Special Moments and Highlights of Our Stay

Guest Names

Dates of Stay

Traveled From

Doodles and Drawings

Message to Host

Favorite Places to Go and Things to Do

Special Moments and Highlights of Our Stay

Guest Names

_____

_____

_____

_____

Dates of Stay

_____

_____

Traveled From

_____

_____

_____

Doodles and Drawings

Message to Host

_____

_____

_____

_____

_____

_____

_____

Favorite Places to Go and Things to Do

_____

_____

_____

_____

Special Moments and Highlights of Our Stay

_____

_____

_____

_____

_____

Guest Names

Dates of Stay

Traveled From

Doodles and Drawings

Message to Host

Favorite Places to Go and Things to Do

Special Moments and Highlights of Our Stay

Guest Names

Dates of Stay

Traveled From

Doodles and Drawings

Message to Host

Favorite Places to Go and Things to Do

Special Moments and Highlights of Our Stay

Guest Names

Dates of Stay

Traveled From

Doodles and Drawings

Message to Host

Favorite Places to Go and Things to Do

Special Moments and Highlights of Our Stay

Guest Names

_____

_____

_____

_____

_____

Dates of Stay

_____

_____

Traveled From

_____

_____

_____

Doodles and Drawings

Message to Host

_____

_____

_____

_____

_____

_____

_____

_____

Favorite Places to Go and Things to Do

_____

_____

_____

_____

_____

Special Moments and Highlights of Our Stay

_____

_____

_____

_____

_____

_____

Guest Names

Dates of Stay

Traveled From

Doodles and Drawings

Message to Host

Favorite Places to Go and Things to Do

Special Moments and Highlights of Our Stay

Guest Names

Dates of Stay

Traveled From

Doodles and Drawings

Message to Host

Favorite Places to Go and Things to Do

Special Moments and Highlights of Our Stay

Guest Names

Dates of Stay

Traveled From

Doodles and Drawings

Message to Host

Favorite Places to Go and Things to Do

Special Moments and Highlights of Our Stay

Guest Names

_____

_____

_____

_____

Dates of Stay

_____

_____

Traveled From

_____

_____

_____

Doodles and Drawings

Message to Host

_____

_____

_____

_____

_____

_____

_____

Favorite Places to Go and Things to Do

_____

_____

_____

_____

_____

Special Moments and Highlights of Our Stay

_____

_____

_____

_____

_____

Guest Names

Dates of Stay

Traveled From

Doodles and Drawings

Message to Host

Favorite Places to Go and Things to Do

Special Moments and Highlights of Our Stay

Guest Names

_____

_____

_____

_____

Dates of Stay

_____

_____

Traveled From

_____

_____

_____

Doodles and Drawings

Message to Host

_____

_____

_____

_____

_____

_____

_____

Favorite Places to Go and Things to Do

_____

_____

_____

_____

_____

_____

Special Moments and Highlights of Our Stay

_____

_____

_____

_____

_____

_____

Guest Names

Dates of Stay

Traveled From

Doodles and Drawings

Message to Host

Favorite Places to Go and Things to Do

Special Moments and Highlights of Our Stay

Guest Names

_____

_____

_____

_____

_____

Dates of Stay

_____

_____

Traveled From

_____

_____

_____

Doodles and Drawings

Message to Host

_____

_____

_____

_____

_____

_____

_____

_____

Favorite Places to Go and Things to Do

_____

_____

_____

_____

_____

_____

Special Moments and Highlights of Our Stay

_____

_____

_____

_____

_____

Guest Names

Dates of Stay

Traveled From

Doodles and Drawings

Message to Host

Favorite Places to Go and Things to Do

Special Moments and Highlights of Our Stay

Guest Names

_____

_____

_____

_____

Dates of Stay

_____

_____

Traveled From

_____

_____

_____

Doodles and Drawings

Message to Host

_____

_____

_____

_____

_____

_____

_____

_____

Favorite Places to Go and Things to Do

_____

_____

_____

_____

_____

_____

Special Moments and Highlights of Our Stay

_____

_____

_____

_____

_____

_____

Guest Names

Dates of Stay

Traveled From

Doodles and Drawings

Message to Host

Favorite Places to Go and Things to Do

Special Moments and Highlights of Our Stay

Guest Names

Dates of Stay

Traveled From

Doodles and Drawings

Message to Host

Favorite Places to Go and Things to Do

Special Moments and Highlights of Our Stay

Guest Names

Dates of Stay

Traveled From

Doodles and Drawings

Message to Host

Favorite Places to Go and Things to Do

Special Moments and Highlights of Our Stay

Guest Names

_____

_____

_____

_____

Dates of Stay

_____

_____

Traveled From

_____

_____

_____

Doodles and Drawings

Message to Host

_____

_____

_____

_____

_____

_____

_____

_____

Favorite Places to Go and Things to Do

_____

_____

_____

_____

_____

_____

Special Moments and Highlights of Our Stay

_____

_____

_____

_____

_____

_____

Guest Names

Message to Host

Dates of Stay

Traveled From

Favorite Places to Go and Things to Do

Doodles and Drawings

Special Moments and Highlights of Our Stay

Guest Names

Dates of Stay

Traveled From

Doodles and Drawings

Message to Host

Favorite Places to Go and Things to Do

Special Moments and Highlights of Our Stay

Guest Names

Dates of Stay

Traveled From

Doodles and Drawings

Message to Host

Favorite Places to Go and Things to Do

Special Moments and Highlights of Our Stay

Guest Names

Dates of Stay

Traveled From

Doodles and Drawings

Message to Host

Favorite Places to Go and Things to Do

Special Moments and Highlights of Our Stay

Guest Names

Dates of Stay

Traveled From

Doodles and Drawings

Message to Host

Favorite Places to Go and Things to Do

Special Moments and Highlights of Our Stay

Guest Names

_____

_____

_____

_____

_____

Dates of Stay

_____

_____

Traveled From

_____

_____

_____

Doodles and Drawings

Message to Host

_____

_____

_____

_____

_____

_____

_____

Favorite Places to Go and Things to Do

_____

_____

_____

_____

_____

_____

Special Moments and Highlights of Our Stay

_____

_____

_____

_____

_____

_____

Guest Names

_____

_____

_____

_____

_____

Dates of Stay

_____

Traveled From

_____

_____

_____

Doodles and Drawings

Message to Host

_____

_____

_____

_____

_____

_____

_____

_____

_____

Favorite Places to Go and Things to Do

_____

_____

_____

_____

_____

Special Moments and Highlights of Our Stay

_____

_____

_____

_____

_____

Guest Names

Dates of Stay

Traveled From

Doodles and Drawings

Message to Host

Favorite Places to Go and Things to Do

Special Moments and Highlights of Our Stay

Guest Names

Dates of Stay

Traveled From

Doodles and Drawings

Message to Host

Favorite Places to Go and Things to Do

Special Moments and Highlights of Our Stay

Guest Names

Dates of Stay

Traveled From

Doodles and Drawings

Message to Host

Favorite Places to Go and Things to Do

Special Moments and Highlights of Our Stay

Guest Names

Dates of Stay

Traveled From

Doodles and Drawings

Message to Host

Favorite Places to Go and Things to Do

Special Moments and Highlights of Our Stay

Guest Names

Dates of Stay

Traveled From

Doodles and Drawings

Message to Host

Favorite Places to Go and Things to Do

Special Moments and Highlights of Our Stay

Guest Names

Dates of Stay

Traveled From

Doodles and Drawings

Message to Host

Favorite Places to Go and Things to Do

Special Moments and Highlights of Our Stay

Guest Names

Dates of Stay

Traveled From

Doodles and Drawings

Message to Host

Favorite Places to Go and Things to Do

Special Moments and Highlights of Our Stay

Guest Names

Dates of Stay

Traveled From

Doodles and Drawings

Message to Host

Favorite Places to Go and Things to Do

Special Moments and Highlights of Our Stay

Guest Names

_____

_____

_____

_____

_____

Dates of Stay

_____

_____

Traveled From

_____

_____

_____

Doodles and Drawings

Message to Host

_____

_____

_____

_____

_____

_____

_____

_____

_____

Favorite Places to Go and Things to Do

_____

_____

_____

_____

_____

_____

Special Moments and Highlights of Our Stay

_____

_____

_____

_____

_____

_____

Guest Names

Dates of Stay

Traveled From

Doodles and Drawings

Message to Host

Favorite Places to Go and Things to Do

Special Moments and Highlights of Our Stay

Guest Names

Dates of Stay

Traveled From

Doodles and Drawings

Message to Host

Favorite Places to Go and Things to Do

Special Moments and Highlights of Our Stay

Guest Names

Dates of Stay

Traveled From

Doodles and Drawings

Message to Host

Favorite Places to Go and Things to Do

Special Moments and Highlights of Our Stay

Guest Names

_____

_____

_____

_____

_____

Dates of Stay

_____

_____

Traveled From

_____

_____

_____

Doodles and Drawings

Message to Host

_____

_____

_____

_____

_____

_____

_____

_____

_____

Favorite Places to Go and Things to Do

_____

_____

_____

_____

_____

_____

Special Moments and Highlights of Our Stay

_____

_____

_____

_____

_____

_____

Guest Names

Message to Host

Dates of Stay

Traveled From

Favorite Places to Go and Things to Do

Doodles and Drawings

Special Moments and Highlights of Our Stay

Guest Names

Dates of Stay

Traveled From

Doodles and Drawings

Message to Host

Favorite Places to Go and Things to Do

Special Moments and Highlights of Our Stay

Guest Names

Dates of Stay

Traveled From

Doodles and Drawings

Message to Host

Favorite Places to Go and Things to Do

Special Moments and Highlights of Our Stay

Guest Names

Dates of Stay

Traveled From

Doodles and Drawings

Message to Host

Favorite Places to Go and Things to Do

Special Moments and Highlights of Our Stay

Guest Names

Dates of Stay

Traveled From

Doodles and Drawings

Message to Host

Favorite Places to Go and Things to Do

Special Moments and Highlights of Our Stay

Guest Names

_____

_____

_____

_____

_____

Dates of Stay

_____

_____

Traveled From

_____

_____

_____

Doodles and Drawings

Message to Host

_____

_____

_____

_____

_____

_____

_____

Favorite Places to Go and Things to Do

_____

_____

_____

_____

_____

_____

Special Moments and Highlights of Our Stay

_____

_____

_____

_____

_____

_____

Guest Names

Dates of Stay

Traveled From

Doodles and Drawings

Message to Host

Favorite Places to Go and Things to Do

Special Moments and Highlights of Our Stay

Guest Names

_____

_____

_____

_____

Dates of Stay

_____

_____

Traveled From

_____

_____

_____

Doodles and Drawings

Message to Host

_____

_____

_____

_____

_____

_____

_____

_____

Favorite Places to Go and Things to Do

_____

_____

_____

_____

_____

Special Moments and Highlights of Our Stay

_____

_____

_____

_____

_____

_____

Guest Names

Dates of Stay

Traveled From

Doodles and Drawings

Message to Host

Favorite Places to Go and Things to Do

Special Moments and Highlights of Our Stay

Guest Names

Dates of Stay

Traveled From

Doodles and Drawings

Message to Host

Favorite Places to Go and Things to Do

Special Moments and Highlights of Our Stay

Guest Names

Dates of Stay

Traveled From

Doodles and Drawings

Message to Host

Favorite Places to Go and Things to Do

Special Moments and Highlights of Our Stay

Guest Names

Dates of Stay

Traveled From

Doodles and Drawings

Message to Host

Favorite Places to Go and Things to Do

Special Moments and Highlights of Our Stay

Guest Names

Dates of Stay

Traveled From

Doodles and Drawings

Message to Host

Favorite Places to Go and Things to Do

Special Moments and Highlights of Our Stay

Guest Names

Dates of Stay

Traveled From

Doodles and Drawings

Message to Host

Favorite Places to Go and Things to Do

Special Moments and Highlights of Our Stay

Guest Names

Dates of Stay

Traveled From

Doodles and Drawings

Message to Host

Favorite Places to Go and Things to Do

Special Moments and Highlights of Our Stay

Guest Names

Dates of Stay

Traveled From

Doodles and Drawings

Message to Host

Favorite Places to Go and Things to Do

Special Moments and Highlights of Our Stay

Guest Names

Dates of Stay

Traveled From

Doodles and Drawings

Message to Host

Favorite Places to Go and Things to Do

Special Moments and Highlights of Our Stay

Guest Names

Dates of Stay

Traveled From

Doodles and Drawings

Message to Host

Favorite Places to Go and Things to Do

Special Moments and Highlights of Our Stay

Guest Names

Dates of Stay

Traveled From

Doodles and Drawings

Message to Host

Favorite Places to Go and Things to Do

Special Moments and Highlights of Our Stay

Guest Names

Dates of Stay

Traveled From

Doodles and Drawings

Message to Host

Favorite Places to Go and Things to Do

Special Moments and Highlights of Our Stay

Guest Names

Dates of Stay

Traveled From

Doodles and Drawings

Message to Host

Favorite Places to Go and Things to Do

Special Moments and Highlights of Our Stay

Guest Names

Dates of Stay

Traveled From

Doodles and Drawings

Message to Host

Favorite Places to Go and Things to Do

Special Moments and Highlights of Our Stay

Guest Names

Dates of Stay

Traveled From

Doodles and Drawings

Message to Host

Favorite Places to Go and Things to Do

Special Moments and Highlights of Our Stay

Guest Names

Dates of Stay

Traveled From

Doodles and Drawings

Message to Host

Favorite Places to Go and Things to Do

Special Moments and Highlights of Our Stay

Guest Names

Dates of Stay

Traveled From

Doodles and Drawings

Message to Host

Favorite Places to Go and Things to Do

Special Moments and Highlights of Our Stay

Made in the USA
Las Vegas, NV
16 August 2023

76193216R00063